NOEL FROM TANZANIA

Story and Photographs by Mary Duda

River Junction
Press

ISBN: 978-0-9972667-1-9 (Cloth)
ISBN: 978-0-9972667-5-7 (Paperback)
ISBN: 978-0-9972667-2-6 (EPUB)
ISBN: 978-0-9972667-3-3 (PDF)
ISBN: 978-0-9972667-4-0 (Mobipocket)

Contact: www.kidsaroundtheglobe.com
         info@kidsaroundtheglobe.com

Dedicated to my Mom and Dad, Catherine and Paul Chen, my husband Jim, our children Joyce, Amy, Phillip, Brian, Lucy, Molly, Carl and Abby, and our grandchildren Kegan, Ellen, Willow, Emma and Will.

Lexile Level 560L, Guided Reading Level L, Interest Level K-5.

Special thanks to publisher Kira Gale, River Junction Press LLC and educational consultant Marla Conn, Read-Ability Inc.

River Junction Press LLC: www.riverjunctionpress.com
Distributed by Independent Publishers Group, Chicago, Illinois www.ipgbook.com
Printed in the United States of America.

Maps from J. Bruce Jones: World of Maps Clip Art, www.gumroad.com
Mount Kilimanjaro photo: www.tanzaniatourism.com

Publisher's Cataloging-In-Publication Data

(Prepared by The Donohue Group, Inc.)

Names: Duda, Mary, author, photographer.

Title: Noel from Tanzania / story and photographs by Mary Duda.

Description: [Omaha, Nebraska] : River Junction Press, [2016] | [Chicago, Illinois] : Independent Publishers Group, [2016] | Series: Children around the world series ; 1 | Interest age level: 006-010. | Summary: "Follow Noel, an 8-year-old boy from Tanzania as he shows you his house, the animals in his yard, and his school. Then learn a magic trick with Noel."-- Provided by publisher.

Identifiers: ISBN 978-0-9972667-1-9 (cloth) | ISBN 978-0-9972667-5-7 (paperback) | ISBN 978-0-9972667-2-6 (ePub) | ISBN 978-0-9972667-3-3 (PDF)

Subjects: LCSH: Children--Tanzania--Juvenile literature. | Children--Tanzania--Pictorial works. | Tanzania--Social life and customs--Juvenile literature. | Tanzania--Social life and customs--Pictorial works. | CYAC: Children--Tanzania--Pictorial works. | Tanzania--Social life and customs--Pictorial works.

Classification: LCC DT438.3 .D84 2016 (print) | LCC DT438.3 (ebook) | DDC 967.8044--dc23

Jambo, my name is Noel.

Jambo means "hello" in Swahili,
the language of Tanzania.

Karibu, welcome to my home.
I live here with my mother and father.

Jambo, my mother says hello.

Here is the kitchen. My mother
doesn't cook food in the kitchen.
She cooks outside over a wood fire.

This is the bathroom. Does it
look like your bathroom?

Only cold water comes out of the shower. You mix it with heated water in a cup and pour it over your head.

This is our yard and our cat.

Does my cat look like the cats
in your country?

We also have cows, chickens and goats.

The cows and goats give us fresh
milk to drink.

The chickens lay eggs for us to eat at breakfast. Can you find the turkey?

This is my school. We study math, reading, Swahili and English. When we are twelve we have to pass a test to go to secondary school.

In school everybody shaves their head and wears a uniform. The girls wear blue skirts and the boys wear beige pants.

Today my friend Jim is teaching me a magic trick. He is showing me how to make a coin disappear.

First Jim holds the coin between his thumb
and forefinger. Then I see him scoop it up
with his left hand. But when he opens his
left hand the coin is not there! Where did
it go? He pretended to take it, but really
dropped it into his right palm.

Now it is my turn to make the
coin disappear. It is hiding in
my pointing hand.

Today is market day. This man is taking
bananas to the market in a hand-made
wheelbarrow. Bananas are harvested green
because they start to split open when they
turn yellow on the banana tree. We have
many different kinds of bananas in Tanzania.
Some are not very sweet and are better for
boiling, frying or baking. Others are sweet
and good to eat raw.

The marketplace is very busy. Do you see the women carrying bananas on their head? You can try carrying something on your head too. If you practice enough you will have better balance and better posture too.

Every week our community holds an auction to raise money for community projects. Fruit, vegetables or animals are sold to the highest bidder. The auctioneer is holding a bag of potatoes grown in our village.

papaya

banana

pineapple

This is a jackfruit. It is good to eat.

This is what we ate for lunch. We had beef stew made from cow stomach, peas and carrots, rice, goat meat, chicken and fruit.

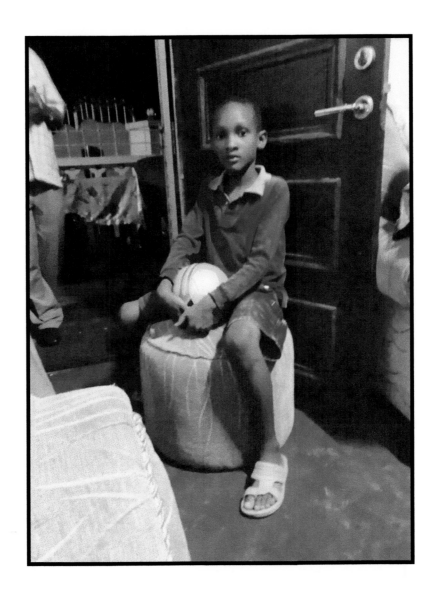

I like to play soccer but there are
no other children where I live.
If you come to Tanzania you can
play soccer with me.

Asante, thank you for reading about me.

If you come visit me in Tanzania, here are some things you could see...

You could go on safari to the world famous Serengeti National Park.

Here is a family of giraffes and Thompson's gazelles.

This lioness is sitting on the road. A very friendly
maribou stork walked right next to our truck.

Here we see a bull elephant and a family of hippopotomuses.

How many storks can you count in this tree?
The zebra is my favorite African animal. What
is your favorite?

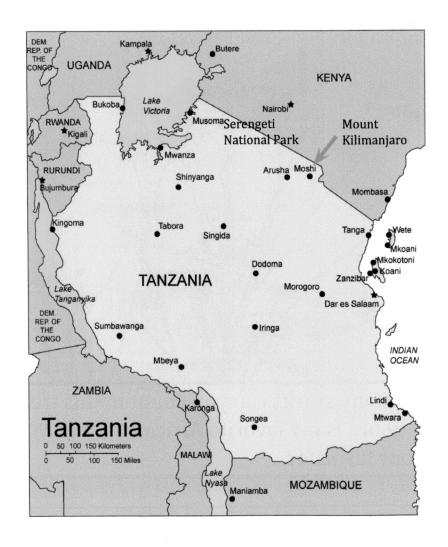

Noel lives in a village on the slopes of
Mount Kilimanjaro, the tallest mountain
in Africa.

Tanzania

Tanzania is located in Africa.

Swahili words used in this book:

asante (Ah-sahn'-tay) - thank you
jambo (Jahm'-bow) - hello
karibu (Kah-ree'-boo) - welcome
safari (Sah-far'-ee) - journey or trip
Serengeti (Ser-ren-get'-tee) - region in northern Tanzania
Swahili (Swah-hee'-lee) - official language of Tanzania

Noel from Tanzania

Follow-up Activities

1. Map skills—Print out a blank world map from the Kids Around the Globe website. Locate, label and color where you live and where Noel lives. How far are you from Tanzania? How long would it take to travel by airplane? Is there another way to get to Tanzania? Can you walk, drive or take a train? Explain.

2. Go back to the text—What did you learn about Noel? Create a "Main Idea and Supporting Details Chart."

3. Compare and contrast the life of Noel with your own life. Include details from the chart above (school, family, sports, foods, housing, language, pets, clothing, community, location).

4. Do what Noel does!
    Learn a magic trick.
    Present a magic show to the class.
    Write a "how-to" explaining how to create the trick.

5. Create a KWL chart—
    K: What do you Know about Tanzania after reading Noel from Tanzania?
    W: What more do you Want to know?
    L: What have you Learned about Tanzania?

6. Look at the videos on Kids Around the Globe website and write about what you learned.

7. Create a travel brochure for Tanzania.

8. Create a PowerPoint presentation on something you learned about Tanzania.

Holidays	Climate
Animals	Economy
Geography	Language
Foods	Education
Religion	Art

More content available at www.kidsaroundtheglobe.com